Mac 'N' Cheese Co[ok]

A Versatile Collection of Delicious Recipes

by Chloe Tucker

License Notes

Table of Contents

Introduction

Every July 14th, millions across the United States gather to enjoy the National Mac and Cheese day. This dish is made with macaroni pasta, milk or cream, and as many cheeses as you want. It is the mother of all classic comfort food. Mac and Cheese is a standalone dish, but over the years, chefs have tried their hands to not only make it a main course but as starters, dessert, and even snacks.

We know you probably have a recipe in your family, but these are 30 different ways to enjoy a classic with family and friends.

||||||||||||||||||||||||||||||||||||||||||||||||||||||||||||||||||||||||||||||||||

Baked Macaroni and Cheese

It is really easy to make and tastes great. It is a good source of protein, vitamin A, B group vitamins, and calcium.

Duration: 45 minutes

Serving Sizes: 3

Ingredient List:

- Macaroni - 1 (12 ounces) package
- Milk - 2 cups
- Shredded Cheddar cheese - 2 1/2 cups
- Egg - 1
- Butter - 2 tbsp.
- Salt and pepper

||||||||||||||||||||||||||||||||||||||||||||||||||||||||||||||||||||||||||||||||||||||||

Preparation:

At 350°F, let the oven heat up. Oil a baking dish.

Bring the salted water to boil. Stir in macaroni until tender (about 5 minutes).

Beat milk and egg in a cup. Stir in the cheese and butter to milk mixture. Combine well.

Put the macaroni in the baking dish. Spread the cheese liquid on the macaroni. Pour pepper and salt. Mix well.

Place the baking dish in the oven until golden (for 30 minutes).

Wisconsin Five-Cheese Bake

A type of savory twist on the traditional cheese and macaroni. Different cheese layers can be tasted in every bite of this dish

Duration: 25 minutes

Serving Sizes: 12

Ingredient List:

- Elbow macaroni - 1 (16 ounces) package
- Swiss cheese - 1 cup
- Shredded provolone cheese - 1 cup
- Sour cream - 1/2 cup
- Chopped parsley - 1 tbsp.
- Shredded mozzarella cheese - 1 cup
- Grated Parmesan cheese - 1 cup
- Ricotta cheese - 1/2 cup
- Cream - half cup
- Italian seasoning - 1/2 tsp.
- Garlic salt - half tsp.

||||||||||||||||||||||||||||||||||||||||||||||||||||||||||||||||||||||||||||||||||||||

Preparation:

At 400°F, let the oven heat up. Lightly oil a baking dish. Boil salted water in a pot. Stir in the macaroni and boil until soft (for 8 minutes). Sieve.

Take a mixing bowl and stir in mozzarella cheese, Provolone cheese, Swiss cheese, and Parmesan cheese. Reserve the half cup of cream and put it aside for the topping. Take another mixing bowl and put ricotta cheese, heavy cream, and sour cream. Sprinkle parsley, garlic salt, and Italian seasoning.

Add heavy cream batter and macaroni to the mixing bowl. Stir in the cheeses. Mix well. Stir in the baking dish. Spread reserved cheese on it.

Place it in the oven until the cheese melts (for 10 minutes).

Macaroni and Cheese V

It is perfect. You can make it more or less cheesy, depending on your taste.

Duration: 50 minutes

Serving Sizes: 6

Ingredient List:

- Breadcrumbs - 3/4 cup
- Macaroni - 8 ounces
- Onion (minced) - 1
- Salt and pepper
- Milk - 1 1/2 cups
- Butter - 2 tbsp.
- Butter - 2 tbsp.
- All-purpose flour - 1 tbsp.
- Mustard - 1/4 tsp.
- Shredded Cheddar cheese - 2 cups

||||||||||||||||||||||||||||||||||||||||||||||||||||||||||||||||||||||||||||||||||||

Preparation:

At 350°F, let the oven heat up. Lightly oil a casserole dish. Put breadcrumbs in a bowl and heat the butter. Put it aside.

Boil the salted water in a pot. Stir in the macaroni and cook until tender about 10 minutes. Sieve. Put it in a casserole dish.

Heat 2 tbsp. of the butter in a pan. Add minced onion and heat until tender (for 5 minutes).

Add flour, dry mustard, pepper, and salt until well mixed. Add milk and simmer. Stir until it gets thick (for 10 minutes). Remove from the heat and add Cheddar cheese until it melts. Put the cheese sauce on the macaroni. Pour buttered breadcrumbs.

Place it in the oven until golden (for 20 minutes).

Easy Mac and Cheese Muffins

It takes a delighted approach to the mac and cheese. Children can eat this just like a treat.

Duration: 55 minutes

Serving Sizes: 12

Ingredient List:

- Elbow macaroni - 2 cups
- Egg - 1
- Shredded Cheddar cheese – 1 and 1/2 cups
- Seasoned breadcrumbs - 1/2 cup
- Salt - 1/2 tsp.
- Butter - 1 tbsp.
- Milk - 1 cup
- Mozzarella cheese, shredded – 1 and 1/2 cups
- Olive oil - 2 tsp.

‖‖

Preparation:

At 350°F, let the oven heat up. Lightly oil the muffin tin. Take a mixing bowl and stir in breadcrumbs, salt, and olive oil. Put it aside.

Boil the salted water in a pot. Stir in macaroni and boil until tender (for 8 minutes). Turn off the heat and sieve the macaroni.

Put it in the pan and add the egg and butter. Reserve a half-cup of Cheddar cheese. Add cheddar cheese, mozzarella cheese, and milk in the pasta. Put it in the muffin tin. Spread the remaining cheese and the mixture.

Place it in the oven for about 30 minutes.

Creamy Macaroni and Cheese

Macaroni and cheese is delicious superfood. It is a kids' favorite, and adults like it too.

Duration: 40 minutes

Serving Sizes: 10

Ingredient List:

- Salt - 1 tbsp.
- Evaporated milk - 2 (12 fluid ounces) cans
- Butter - 3 tbsp.
- Dijon mustard - 1 1/2 tbsp.
- Ground black pepper
- Elbow pasta - 1 pound
- Chicken broth - 1 cup
- Flour - 1/3 cup
- Grated Parmesan cheese - 1/2 cup
- Grated cheddar cheese - 1 pound

|||||||||||||||||||||||||||||||||||||||||||||||||||||||||||||||||||||||||||||||||||||||||||||||||||||

Preparation:

Boil water in a pot. Stir in the pasta and salt until tender. Sieve.

Microwave chicken broth and milk in a bowl. Heat the butter in a pot. Add the flour and stir in the milk mixture. Stir until it gets thickened (for 4 minutes). Add the mustard, pepper, and Parmesan. Remove from the heat and put in cheddar.

Pour the drained pasta into the sauce. Mix all together well.

Ginny's Cheesy Macaroni

So easy even a husband can do it. It takes 1 hour and 10 minutes to prepare.

Duration: 1 hour 10 minutes

Serving Sizes: 6

Ingredient List:

- Margarine - 3 tbsp.
- Salt - 1 tsp.
- Cheddar cheese - 1 (8 ounces) package
- Macaroni - 2 1/2 cups
- Black pepper - 1 tsp.
- Milk - 4 cups

||||||||||||||||||||||||||||||||||||||||||||||||||||||||||||||||||||||||||||||||||||||||||

Preparation:

At 350°F, let the oven heat up.

Grease a baking dish and place it in the oven so that it melts. Put the macaroni, pepper, and salt.

Pour the cheese over the macaroni. Pour the milk onto it.

Place it in the oven for about 60 minutes.

Homemade Baked Macaroni and Cheese

My friend made this recipe. It is a favorite in my family.

Duration: 1 hour 15 minutes

Serving Sizes: 6

Ingredient List:

- Elbow macaroni - 2 1/2 cups
- All-purpose flour - 1/4 cup
- Milk - 4 cups
- Butter - 1/4 cup
- Salt - 1/2 tsp.
- Cheddar cheese - 1 pound
- Buttery round crackers - 1 sleeve

‖‖

Preparation:

At 350°F, let the oven heat up.

Boil the salted water in a pot (high heat). Add macaroni and boil until the macaroni gets soft (for 8 minutes). Sieve.

Heat a quarter cup of the butter in a pan. Add the salt and flour. Cook for about 2 minutes. Pour milk and heat until the mixture gets thick (for 5 minutes).

Remove from the heat and add the cheese until it gets melted. Stir in macaroni and mix. Put the mixture in a baking dish. Take a bowl and stir in the remaining butter and crackers. Spread it over the macaroni.

Place the baking dish in the oven until it gets light brown (for 45 minutes).

Slow Cooker Mac and Cheese

It is a creamy, comforting meal. It is always a big hit. It is superb for large family gatherings.

Duration: 3 hours 25 minutes

Serving Sizes: 12

Ingredient List:

- Elbow macaroni - 1 (16 ounces) package
- Salt and ground black pepper
- Evaporated milk - 1 (5 ounces) can
- Whole milk - 2 cups
- Paprika (optional) - 1 pinch
- Butter - 1/2 cup
- Shredded cheddar cheese (divided) - 1 (16 ounces) package
- Eggs - 2
- Condensed cheddar cheese soup - 1 (10.75 ounces) can

||||||||||||||||||||||||||||||||||||||||||||||||||||||||||||||||||||||||||||||||||||||||||||||||||||

Preparation:

Boil the salted water in a large pot. Stir in the elbow macaroni and boil until tender (for 8 minutes). Sieve and put it in the slow cooker.

Put butter in the pasta and mix well. Sprinkle the pepper and salt. Pour 1/2 of Cheddar cheese on the pasta and mix.

Take a mixing bowl and beat the evaporated milk until the mixture gets smooth. Pour it into the pasta mixture.

Take another bowl and beat the Cheddar cheese soup and milk until soft. Pour it into the pasta mixture. Pour the remaining cheese over the pasta mixture and sprinkle the paprika.

Heat it on low for about 3 hours.

Old Fashioned Mac and Cheese

It is a classic recipe for macaroni and cheese. The children will love this.

Duration: 1 hour 5 minutes

Serving Sizes: 7

Ingredient List:

- Elbow macaroni - 2 cups
- All-purpose flour - 2 tbsp.
- Onion (minced) - 1/4
- Processed cheese food - 1/4 pound
- Shredded Swiss cheese - 1/4 pound
- Butter - 4 tbsp.
- Milk - 2 cups
- Salt and pepper
- Shredded cheddar cheese - 1/4 pound

||||||||||||||||||||||||||||||||||||||||||||||||||||||||||||||||||||||||||||||||||

Preparation:

At 350°F, let the oven heat up.

Boil elbow macaroni in the salted water. Drain.

Heat butter in a pan. Add flour until it becomes a smooth paste. Stir in milk and let it boil. Turn off the heat and put it aside.

Put the macaroni in a baking dish. Spread 1/2 grated onion, 1/2 each of cheeses, 1/2 salt, and 1/2 pepper. Repeat it once more. Now, spread white sauce on it. Sprinkle butter over it.

Cover the dish and place it in the oven at 350°F (about 45 minutes).

Homemade Mac and Cheese

This is a yummy rich mac and cheese. Serve it with a salad for a great meatless dinner.

Duration: 50 minutes

Serving Sizes: 4

Ingredient List:

- Elbow macaroni - 8 ounces
- Grated Parmesan cheese - 1/2 cup
- Butter - 1/4 cup
- Butter - 2 tbsp.
- Paprika - 1 pinch
- Shredded Cheddar cheese - 2 cups
- Milk - 3 cups
- All-purpose flour - 2 1/2 tbsp.
- Breadcrumbs - 1/2 cup

||||||||||||||||||||||||||||||||||||||||||||||||||||||||||||||||||||||||||||||||||||||||||

Preparation:

Boil the macaroni in lightly salted water. Sieve.

Take a pan and heat the butter. Add the flour. Pour the milk into the roux. Add the cheeses. Heat until the cheeses melt, and the sauce gets thickened. Add the macaroni to a baking dish and put the sauce on it. Mix.

Heat the butter in a pan. Stir in the breadcrumbs until they get golden. Pour it on the macaroni. Sprinkle with paprika.

Place the baking dish in the oven at 350°F (for 30 minutes).

Instant Pot Mac and Cheese with Ham and Peas

Prepare mac and cheese at home for dinner. The ham, hot sauce, and peas add more taste to the classic mac and cheese.

Duration: 44 minutes

Serving Sizes: 6

Ingredient List:

- Water - 4 cups
- Mustard powder - 1 tsp.
- Hot sauce (optional) - 1 tsp.
- Whole milk - 1/3 cup
- 2% milk Cheddar cheese - 2 cups
- Diced cooked ham - 1 cup
- Salt and black pepper
- Elbow macaroni - 1 (16 ounces) package
- Salt - 1 tsp.
- Evaporated milk - 1 (12 fluid ounces) can
- Unsalted butter - 2 tbsp.
- Monterey Jack cheese - 1 cup
- Peas - 1/2 cup

|||||||||||||||||||||||||||||||||||||||||||||||||||||||||||||||||||||||||||||||||

Preparation:

Put the water, hot sauce, elbow macaroni, salt, and mustard powder in a pressure cooker. Cover the pressure cooker tightly. Set the timer for about 4 minutes. Select the high pressure following the directions of the manufacturer (about 15 minutes).

Remove the lid and set it to Low. Stir the macaroni to avoid clumps.

Put the evaporated milk, butter, and milk in the pot. Stir in the Monterey Jack cheese and Cheddar cheese. Add the peas and ham. Sprinkle the pepper and salt.

Mac and Cheese II

This recipe is very simple to prepare! It can be a side dish with meatloaf and stewed tomatoes.

Duration: 1 hour 5 minutes

Serving Sizes: 4

Ingredient List:

- Elbow macaroni - 8 ounces
- All-purpose flour - 1/4 cup
- Shredded cheddar cheese - 1 cup
- Butter - 2 tbsp.
- Milk - 2 cups
- Processed cheese food - 8 ounces

||||||||||||||||||||||||||||||||||||||||||||||||||||||||||||||||||||||||||||||||||||||||||||||||

Preparation:

Boil the salted water in a pot and stir in the elbow macaroni until tender. Sieve.

Heat the butter in a pan. Add the flour. Pour the milk and heat it until it gets thickened for 7 minutes. Stir in the cheeses and heat until it melts.

Take a bowl and combine cheese mixture and pasta. Mix well.

Pour it into a casserole dish. Place it in the oven at 350°F (about 30 minutes).

Baked Mac and Cheese for One

This is a quick, easy-to-make, and filling meal. I cook it in a soup crock.

Duration: 30 minutes

Serving Sizes: 1

Ingredient List:

- Macaroni pasta - 3 tbsp.
- All-purpose flour - 1 tbsp.
- Pepper - 1 pinch
- Milk - 1/2 cup
- Ground mustard - 1/8 tsp.
- Hot sauce - 1 dash
- Shredded cheddar cheese - 1 tbsp.
- Butter - 1 tbsp.
- Salt - 1/4 tsp.
- Onion powder - 1/8 tsp.
- Shredded cheddar cheese - 1/3 cup
- Worcestershire sauce - 1 dash
- Breadcrumbs - 1 tsp.

‖‖‖

Preparation:

At 400°F, let the oven heat up. Lightly grease a crock or a baking dish.

Boil the water in a pot. Add macaroni to the boiling water and cook until tender (for 8 minutes). Sieve the macaroni and set it aside.

Heat the butter in a pan over medium heat. Put flour, milk, salt, onion powder, and pepper. Stir until it gets soft. Cook it for 2 minutes. Decrease the heat of the stove to low. Add 1/3 cup of the cheese, hot sauce, mustard, and Worcestershire sauce. Put macaroni in it. Put macaroni and cheese in the dish. Sprinkle the breadcrumbs as well as 1 tbsp. of the cheddar cheese.

Place it in the oven until golden from the top (for 10 minutes).

Allie's Mac n Cheese

It is very cheesy! I am sure you would like it. You will be addicted to it.

Duration: 1 hour

Serving Sizes: 6

Ingredient List:

- Elbow macaroni - 1 (8 ounces) package
- All-purpose flour - 5 tbsp.
- Salt and pepper
- Cubed ham - 1/4 pound
- Mozzarella cheese - 5 ounces
- Paprika to taste
- Butter - 5 tbsp.
- Warm milk - 1 quart
- Cayenne pepper - 1 pinch
- Cheddar cheese - 5 ounces
- Monterey jack cheese - 5 ounces

‖‖

Preparation:

At 350°F, let the oven heat up. Lightly oil a baking dish. Boil the salted water in a pot. Stir in the pasta and cook until tender (about 10 minutes). Sieve.

In a pan, heat the butter. Put the flour. Cook for 2 minutes. Stir constantly. Add milk and mix well. Let it boil. Decrease the heat. Put the salt, cayenne, and pepper. Stir frequently until the sauce gets thick.

Turn off the heat and add cheddar, ham, mozzarella, and jack. Mix pasta and sauce. Combine well. Put it in the baking dish. Sprinkle with paprika. Place it in the oven for 1 hour.

Cauliflower Mac-N-Cheese

It is a simple mac-n-cheese. It takes just 30 minutes to prepare.

Duration: 30 minutes

Serving Sizes: 4

Ingredient List:

- Elbow macaroni - 1 1/2 cups
- Cooking spray
- All-purpose flour - 1 tbsp.
- Shredded Cheddar cheese - 1 1/2 cups
- Salt - 1/2 tsp.
- Cauliflower florets - 1/2 cup
- Olive oil - 1 tbsp.
- Milk - 1/2 cup
- Cream cheese - 1/2 (8 ounces) package
- Ground black pepper - 1/8 tsp.

IIIIIIIIIIIIIIIIIIIIIIIIIIIIIIIIIIIIIIIIIIIIIIIIIIIIIIIIIIIIIIIIIIIIIIIIIIIIIIIIIIIIIIIIIIIIIIIIIIIIIII

Preparation:

Boil the salted water in a pot. Stir in the elbow macaroni and cook until soft (for 8 minutes). Sieve the macaroni.

Put the steamer in a pan. Pour the water into the steamer below its bottom. Let the water boil. Stir in the cauliflower and heat until soft (for 5 minutes). Now, blend the cauliflower until it gets smooth.

Heat the oil in a pan over medium heat. Stir in the flour and oil. Cook until the paste gets thickened (for 2 minutes). Pour in the milk and cook until the mixture gets thick (for 4 minutes).

Put the cauliflower, pepper, Cheddar cheese, salt, and cream cheese in the milk mixture. Cook until the sauce gets smooth. Put the macaroni in the sauce. Mix well.

Baked Macaroni and Cheese from Mom

Quick macaroni, tangy cheese soup, milk, and wonderful Colby cheese!

Duration: 45 minutes

Serving Sizes: 6

Ingredient List:

- Shredded Colby cheese - 1 pound
- Macaroni - 1 (16 ounces) package
- Milk - 1 cup
- Cheddar cheese soup - 1 (10.75 ounces) can

||||||||||||||||||||||||||||||||||||||||||||||||||||||||||||||||||||||||||||||||||||||||||||||

Preparation:

At 350°F, let the oven heat up. Boil salted water in a pot. Stir in the pasta and cook until tender (for 10 minutes). Sieve.

Put the macaroni in a casserole dish. Add the milk and cheese soup. Mix well. Put in the shredded Colby.

Place it in the oven for 30 minutes.

Baked Macaroni and Cheese III

This dish would make your guest beg for the second. My whole family loves it.

Duration: 45 minutes

Serving Sizes: 10

Ingredient List:

- Elbow macaroni - 1 (16 ounces) package
- Eggs - 2
- Seasoning salt - 1 tsp.
- Shredded cheddar cheese - 1 1/2 cups
- Butter - 1 tbsp.
- Evaporated milk - 1/2 cup
- Sour cream - 1 (8 ounces) container
- Black pepper - 1/2 tsp.
- Grated parmesan cheese - 1/2 cup

‖‖‖

Preparation:

At 350°F, let the oven heat up.

Boil the salted water in a pot. Stir in the pasta and boil until tender (for 10 minutes). Sieve the pasta and put it aside.

Take a mixing bowl and stir in the milk, pepper, eggs, seasoning salt, and sour cream. Put the macaroni, shredded cheddar cheese, and eggs mixture in the baking pan. Pour the Parmesan cheese as well as butter on top.

Place it in the oven until golden from the top (for 30 minutes).

Dijon Mac n Cheese

It contains cream cheese sauce and cheesy cheddar. There is Dijon on the Macaroni, and it is sprinkled with breadcrumbs. It is super yummy.

Duration: 40 minutes

Serving Sizes: 6

Ingredient List:

- Macaroni - 7 ounces
- All-purpose flour - 3 tbsp.
- Cream cheese - 1 (8 ounces) package
- Black pepper - 1/2 tsp.
- Shredded Cheddar cheese - 2 cups
- Butter - 2 tbsp.
- Butter - 1/4 cup
- Milk - 2 cups
- Salt - 1/2 tsp.
- Dijon mustard - 2 tsp.
- Breadcrumbs - 1 cup
- Chopped parsley - 2 tbsp.

||||||||||||||||||||||||||||||||||||||||||||||||||||||||||||||||||||||||||||||||||||||||||

Preparation:

At 400°F, let the oven heat up.

Boil the salted water in a pot. Stir in the macaroni pasta. Let it boil for 10 minutes. Sieve.

Heat the butter in a pan and add the flour. Heat until smooth (for 1 minute). Add the milk, Dijon mustard, cream cheese, pepper, and salt. Cook until the sauce gets thick. Stir in the mac n cheese.

Put it in the casserole dish. Put the breadcrumbs, parsley, and butter in a mixing bowl. Put it on the mac n cheese. Place it in the oven until light brown (for 20 minutes).

Gluten-Free Mac-n-Cheese

Mascarpone makes this cheesy pasta extra creamy. The addition of potato starch thickens the sauce without the flour.

Duration: 30 minutes

Serving Sizes: 6

Ingredient List:

- Gluten-free pasta - 12 ounces
- Onion (chopped) - 1/2
- Evaporated milk - 1 (12 fluid ounces) can
- Mascarpone cheese - 1/3 cup
- Butter - 6 tbsp.
- Potato starch - 1/4 cup
- Shredded Cheddar cheese - 2 cups
- Hot sauce (optional) - 3 dashes

||||||||||||||||||||||||||||||||||||||||||||||||||||||||||||||||||||||||||||||||||||||||||||

Preparation:

Boil the salted water in a pot. Stir in the pasta and cook until it gets soft (for 7 minutes). Sieve the pasta. Reserve 1/2 cup of the cooking liquid. Put the pasta in a bowl.

Heat the butter in a pan. Stir in the onion and heat until tender (for 3 minutes). Put the potato starch and heat until it dissolves (for 1 minute). Add the evaporated milk to the onion mixture. Mix well. Simmer the sauce and turn off the heat.

Add the Cheddar cheese, hot sauce, and mascarpone cheese to the sauce.

Combine the cheese sauce and pasta.

All Day Macaroni and Cheese

It takes 6 hours to cook, but just a few minutes to prepare!

Duration: 6 hours 25 minutes

Serving Sizes: 6

Ingredient List:

- Elbow macaroni - 8 ounces
- Evaporated milk - 1 (12 fluid ounces) can
- Eggs - 2
- Ground black pepper - 1/2 tsp.
- Shredded cheddar cheese - 4 cups
- Milk - 1 1/2 cups
- Salt - 1 tsp.

||||||||||||||||||||||||||||||||||||||||||||||||||||||||||||||||||||||||||||||||||||||||||

Preparation:

Boil macaroni in water until tender (for 10 minutes). Sieve.

Take a mixing bowl and stir in cooked macaroni, pepper, Cheddar cheese, salt, evaporated milk, eggs, and milk. Put it in a greased slow cooker.

Cover the cooker and heat on low for about 6 hours. Serve hot.

Kicked Up Mac and Cheese

This is a super yummy recipe for mac and cheese. My mother taught me to cook this.

Duration: 1 hour 10 minutes

Serving Sizes: 8

Ingredient List:

- Rotelle pasta - 1 1/2 cups
- All-purpose flour - 1/4 cup
- Dry mustard - 1 tsp.
- Ground white pepper - 1/2 tsp.
- Pepper jack cheese - 1 cup
- Parmesan cheese - 1/2 cup
- Chili powder - 2 tsp.
- Butter (divided) - 4 tbsp.
- Whole milk - 3 cups
- Salt - 3/4 tsp.
- Hot pepper sauce - 3 tsp.
- Cheddar cheese - 1 1/2 cups
- Breadcrumbs - 1/3 cup

Preparation:

At 375°F, let the oven heat up.

Boil salted water in a large pot. Put the pasta and boil until tender (for 10 minutes). Sieve.

Heat a pan and stir in the 2 tbsp. of butter to melt. Add the flour and heat for 1 minute. Pour the milk, hot sauce, mustard, pepper, and salt. Let it boil and stir constantly (for 1 minute). Turn off the heat and add the pepper jack, Parmesan, and Cheddar. Stir in the pasta. Stir in the baking dish.

Heat the remaining butter. Put the chili powder and breadcrumbs. Put it on the macaroni mixture.

Place the baking dish in the oven (for 30 minutes).

Mouse's Macaroni and Cheese

The cheesiest and easiest recipe I know. It is terrific. I love this.

Duration: 50 minutes

Serving Sizes: 6

Ingredient List:

- Elbow macaroni - 1 1/2 cups
- All-purpose flour - 2 tbsp.
- Ground black pepper - 1 tsp.
- American cheese - 8 ounces
- Seasoned breadcrumbs - 1/4 cup
- Butter - 1/4 cup
- Mustard powder - 1 tsp.
- Milk - 2 cups
- Processed cheese food - 8 ounces

‖‖

Preparation:

At 400°F, let the oven heat up. Lightly grease a casserole dish. Boil the salted water in a pot. Stir in the macaroni and let boil until tender (for 6 minutes). Sieve.

Heat the butter in a pan. Add flour, pepper, and mustard powder until soft. Pour milk and stir constantly. Stir in American as well as processed cheeses. Cook until the sauce gets thickened and soft.

Sieve the noodles. Put the noodles in cheese sauce. Pour this mixture into the casserole dish. Pour the breadcrumbs on their top.

Cover and place it in the oven until the sauce gets thickened (for 25 minutes).

Mom's Favorite Baked Mac and Cheese

I made it for my mother. It is now her favorite macaroni and cheese.

Duration: 1 hour 5 minutes

Serving Sizes: 6

Ingredient List:

- Butter - 2 tbsp.
- All-purpose flour - 2 tbsp.
- Salt - 3/4 tsp.
- Ground black pepper - 1/4 tsp.
- Shredded Cheddar cheese - 2 cups
- Chopped onion - 1/4 cup
- Milk - 2 cups
- Dry mustard - 1/2 tsp.
- Elbow macaroni - 1 (8 ounces) package
- Processed American cheese - 1 (8 ounces) package

||||||||||||||||||||||||||||||||||||||||||||||||||||||||||||||||||||||||||||||||||||||||||||||||||

Preparation:

At 350°F, let the oven heat up.

Heat the butter in a pan. Fry the onion (about 2 minutes). Add the flour and heat (for 1 minute). Put milk, pepper, salt, and mustard. Cook until the mixture gets thickened.

Boil the salted water in a pot. Stir in the macaroni and boil until it gets tender (for 10 minutes).

Put American and Cheddar cheeses in milk mixture until the cheese gets melted. Pour macaroni as well as cheese sauce into a baking dish.

Place it in the oven for about 30 minutes.

Chuck's Favorite Mac and Cheese

Cottage cheese and sour cream are the unique ingredients in this macaroni and cheese recipe.

Duration: 55 minutes

Serving Sizes: 6

Ingredient List:

- Elbow macaroni - 1 (8 ounces) package
- Curd cottage cheese - 1 (12 ounces) container
- Grated Parmesan cheese - 1/4 cup
- Breadcrumbs - 1 cup
- Shredded Cheddar cheese - 1 (8 ounces) package
- Sour cream - 1 (8 ounces) container
- Salt and pepper
- Butter - 1/4 cup

||||||||||||||||||||||||||||||||||||||||||||||||||||||||||||||||||||||||||||||||||||||||||||

Preparation:

At 350°F, let the oven heat up. Boil the salted water in a pot. Stir in the pasta and boil until tender. Sieve.

Take a baking dish and add the macaroni, pepper, shredded Cheddar cheese, salt, cottage cheese, Parmesan cheese, and sour cream. Take a mixing bowl and stir in melted butter and breadcrumbs. Spread the topping on the macaroni mixture.

Place it in the oven until golden for 30 minutes.

Buffalo Chicken Mac and Cheese

Buffalo chicken mac and cheese is great. It is super yummy.

Duration: 35 minutes

Serving Sizes: 8

Ingredient List:

- Elbow macaroni - 1 (16 ounces) package
- Butter - 6 tbsp.
- Milk - 3 cups
- Cheddar cheese - 2 cups
- Hot sauce - 1/2 cup
- Rotisserie-roasted chicken - 1
- All-purpose flour - 6 tbsp.
- Black pepper (ground) - 1 pinch
- Monterey Jack cheese - 2 cups
- Gorgonzola cheese - 1/2 cup

||||||||||||||||||||||||||||||||||||||||||||||||||||||||||||||||||||||||||||||||||||||

Preparation:

Boil the salted water in a pot. Stir in the macaroni and cook until soft (for 8 minutes). Sieve the macaroni.

Cut the legs as well as wings off the rotisserie chicken. Chop the dark meat and make small pieces.

Heat the butter in the Dutch oven. Add the flour and stir until it gets thickened. Heat until light brown (for 1 minute). Add the milk and stir for 5 minutes. Cook the sauce until it gets smooth (for 1 minute). Decrease the heat of the stove and sprinkle black pepper.

Add the Monterey Jack cheese and Cheddar to the sauce until the cheeses melt. Add the hot sauce. Stir in the blue cheese, macaroni, and chicken. Mix all together well.

Classic Macaroni and Cheese

This is the classic baked Mac and Cheese. You can add sun-dried tomatoes.

Duration: 1 hour 10 minutes

Serving Sizes: 6

Ingredient List:

- Macaroni - 1 (16 ounces) package
- Butter - 1 tbsp.
- Evaporated milk - 1 (12 fluid ounces) can
- Cheddar cheese (sliced) - 1 pound
- Salt and pepper

||||||||||||||||||||||||||||||||||||||||||||||||||||||||||||||||||||||||||||||||||||||||||||||||

Preparation:

At 375°F, let the oven heat up. Boil the salted water in a pot. Stir in the pasta and boil until tender (for 10 minutes). Sieve.

Lightly oil a casserole dish. Put the cooked macaroni and then cheese slices. Sprinkle butter and pepper. Make 3 more layers. Top with evaporated milk.

Bake until golden from the top (for 1 hour).

Ham and Cheese Bowties

Duration: 45 minutes

Serving Sizes: 6

Ingredient List:

- Farfalle (bow-tie) pasta - 8 ounces
- Garlic (minced) - 1 clove
- Salt - 1/2 tsp.
- Milk - 2 cups
- Shredded Colby cheese - 2 1/2 cups
- Grated Parmesan cheese - 1/4 cup
- Butter - 1/4 cup
- All-purpose flour - 1/4 cup
- Ground black pepper - 1/8 tsp.
- Prepared mustard - 1/2 tsp.
- Cooked ham - 4 ounces

‖‖‖

Preparation:

At 350°F, let the oven heat up.

Boil the salted water in a pot. Stir in the pasta and boil until tender (for 10 minutes). Sieve.

Heat the butter in a pan. Fry the garlic (for 30 seconds). Add the flour, pepper, and salt. Cook until soft. Add milk and stir constantly. Let it boil for about 1 minute. Add Colby and mustard. Cook until the cheese melts. Turn off the heat and add ham and pasta.

Put it in the baking dish. Pour the Parmesan.

Place it in the oven until golden (for 20 minutes).

Cafeteria Macaroni and Cheese

This is an old-fashioned comfort food recipe. This is a hit in my family.

Duration: 50 minutes

Serving Sizes: 6

Ingredient List:

- Macaroni - 8 ounces
- Ground mustard - 1 1/2 tsp.
- Salt - 3/4 tsp.
- Butter - 1 1/2 tbsp.
- Breadcrumbs - 1/2 cup
- Paprika - 1/2 tsp.
- Milk - 1 1/2 cups
- Worcestershire sauce - 1 tsp.
- Hot pepper sauce - 1 dash
- Shredded Cheddar cheese - 3 1/2 cups
- Butter - 2 tbsp.

‖‖

Preparation:

At 350°F, let the oven heat up. Lightly oil a casserole dish.

Boil the salted water in a pot. Put the macaroni and boil until tender (for 10 minutes). Sieve and set aside.

Boil milk in a pan. Add the mustard, hot sauce, Worcestershire sauce, and salt. Mix well and put it aside.

Add 1 1/2 tbsp. of the butter as well as 3 cups of cheese to macaroni. Put milk mixture on it. Pour it into the baking dish. Top with the left half cup of the cheddar. Combine butter with breadcrumbs and pour on top. Season with paprika.

Place it in the oven for about 30 minutes. Then, put it under a broiler (about 2 minutes).

Simple Macaroni and Cheese

It is a very quick and easy fix to a delicious side dish. This recipe is cheap and delicious.

Duration: 30 minutes

Serving Sizes: 4

Ingredient List:

- Elbow macaroni - 1 (8 ounces) box
- All-purpose flour - 1/4 cup
- Ground black pepper
- Shredded cheddar cheese - 2 cups
- Butter - 1/4 cup
- Salt - 1/2 tsp.
- Milk - 2 cups

||||||||||||||||||||||||||||||||||||||||||||||||||||||||||||||||||||||||||||||||||||||

Preparation:

Boil the salted water in a pot. Add the elbow macaroni to the water and stir occasionally. Cook until tender for 8 minutes. Sieve and set aside.

Heat the butter in a pan. Put flour, pepper, and salt. Heat it for 5 minutes. Add the milk to the butter mixture until the mixture gets smooth (for 5 minutes). Combine the Cheddar cheese with the milk mixture and mix until the cheese melts (for 4 minutes).

Combine the macaroni with cheese sauce and mix well.

Restaurant-Style Mac and Cheese

It is a superb restaurant-style macaroni with cheese. It is easy and quick to make.

Duration: 25 minutes

Serving Sizes: 4

Ingredient List:

- Macaroni - 1 1/2 cups
- Cheddar cheese (shredded) - 1/2 cup
- Salt to taste
- Processed cheese - 6 ounces
- Heavy cream - 2 tbsp.

||||||||||||||||||||||||||||||||||||||||||||||||||||||||||||||||||||||||||||||||||||||||

Preparation:

Pour water and salt into a pot and let it boil. Stir in the pasta and boil until tender (about 10 minutes). Sieve it.

Again, put the pasta in the pot. Add the processed cheese, cream, and Cheddar cheese until the cheeses get melted. Sprinkle the salt.

Biography

For decades, this beautiful actress graced our screens with her incredible talent and performance in movies that captivated the script and emotions of the viewers. Well, life rarely goes as planned, but we should always make the best out of it, like Chloe.

Originally from the bubbly city of Los Angeles, she has moved from the movie industry into the food scene. Her role in Mama Mia ignited her passion for food. She has taken the New York scene by surprise. Charmed by the unique regions she had visited, the delicious delicacies she tasted, her uncanny appreciation for flavors, ingredients, and cooking techniques have continued to wow customers wide and far.

However, as mentioned, she started as an actress. Breaking into the food scene was easy because she had contacts and connections, but satisfying clients was a different ball game. Over the years, she has mastered the food scenes and unique flavors clients seek. Today, her clients can attest to the high-quality food from her restaurants.

The New York food scene is a jungle that only the strong dare to tread. However, she was a passionate student and learned the tricks and tips, and slowly set her passion for delivering excellent tastes to all who sought them.

An Author's Afterthought

Did you like my book? I pondered it severely before releasing this book. Although the response has been overwhelming, it is always pleasing to see, read or hear a new comment. Thank you for reading this and I would love to hear your honest opinion about it. Furthermore, many people are searching for a unique book, and your feedback will help me gather the right books for my reading audience.

Thanks!

Chloe Tucker

Printed in Great Britain
by Amazon

23087180R00040